THE IMPACT OF FATHER ABSENCE ON AFRICAN AMERICAN BOYS

DR. GERALD C. HASSELL

Acknowledgments

To my parents, Edwin and Georgia Hassell, who rest in eternal peace, thank you for the seeds you planted in my fertile mind and fueled my thirst for knowledge and desire to serve my community. To my sister, Debbie, your undying support and love have made this book possible. Hannah and Nile, my love for the two of you motivates me to face my fears, strive to be a better father and man. Dr. Brenda Bradley, thank you for your patience, compassion, and being a true inspiration in my life. To my family and friends who encourage me to be better, I thank you for your love and support.

A Salute to Fathers

I salute all the father-absent boys, who are now men and decided to protect, provide, and love your children. Growing up without a father is not easy. Your decision has ended the cycle of father absence and changed the lives of your children for generations to come.

A Salute to Single Mothers

To the single mothers who tirelessly face their daily struggles with dignity and respect. You have the most difficult job in the world. I salute you for your strength, commitment, and love.

Table of Contents

Preface

The goal of this book is to discuss how African American boys from father-absent homes are at an increased risk for living in poverty, developing a poor self-identity, and academic failure when compared to their peers from father present homes. The intent of this book is also to raise awareness of the special needs of this population and to provide some analysis of why a disproportionate number of African American men are considered absent fathers. Finally, rite of passage programs is discussed as a culturally sensitive intervention for reducing the risk factors associated with father absence.

Introduction

The literature defines father absence as a family structure in which the father fails to play a significant role in the emotional, financial, psychological or social wellbeing of his child. The term "father absence" is used as a blanket term to describe the lack of a father figure in a child's life. A father-absent family includes a mother or stepmother with no father, stepfather, or grandfather, present in the home.

The literature describes father absence within the context of divorce, death, or the biological father never establishing a presence in the life of the child. The primary focus of this book is on the latter, the impact of a biological father never having established a presence in the life of his offspring. The typical pattern for the formation of a father-absent home is when a man marries, then exits the home, leaving the mother to raise the children on her own. Another path to a father-absent home that is increasingly becoming more prevalent is for an unmarried woman to have a child and raise that child on her own. This pattern is particularly true in the African American community.

Studies on father absence assert that the offspring from father-absent homes are at a greater risk for teenage pregnancy, living in poverty, juvenile delinquency, high school incompletion, and low self-esteem. The prevalence of father absence in the African American community suggests it may negatively impact millions of children and their families. The current research only provides a descriptive analysis of the risk factors associated with father absence. However, more energy and time should be directed to the development and implementation of culturally specific programs to reduce the impact of father absence in the African American community.

The focus of this book is twofold. I will discuss five risk factors for African American boys from father-absent homes. First, the pervasiveness of father absence and why generations of children remain father-absent is discussed. Second, I look at the socioeconomic impact of father absence. Third, insight is shared about the impact of father absence on mental health, violence and the quality of parental supervision. Forth, I examine how growing up without a father shapes the identity of African American boys. Finally, I will talk about the impact of father absence on high school completion and the inability of the system to educate and support poor children of color.

The second part of the book examines rite of passage programs as a culturally specific intervention for reducing risk factors associated with father absence. A rationale is presented to support the value of using rite of passage programs to reduce the risk factors associated with father absence. Also, a historical and contemporary overview of rites of passage is discussed. This is followed by this author's personal experiences working with rite of passage programs and concludes with recommendations for improving the current community-based programs.

Chapter One

The Pervasiveness of Father Absence in the African American community

The focus of this book is to bring attention to father-absent boys who are raised never knowing or having a relationship with their father. Father-absent boys are at greater risk of living in poverty, dropping out of high school, developing a poor self-identity, incarceration, and becoming absent fathers as well. According to Kids-Count.org data, in 2017, sixty-five percent of African American families with children under the age of eighteen are single-parent households. Ninety-three percent of the single-parent households are maintained by mothers. Father-child heads of households represent only 3% of single-parent families. Two out of three births to African American women less than 35 years of age are now out of wedlock births. Most of these births are to father-absent households. The data suggests that millions of African American children are likely to grow up without a father in their lives.

An appropriate question to ask is why are so many African American men having children and not assuming responsibility for them? Several factors are likely contributors to the increase in father absence in the African American community. First, for more than one hundred years there has been a significant deterioration of the social infrastructure within the African American community. In the past, the role of traditionally strong institutions such as the Black Church, African American owned businesses, and locally supported schools were to reinforce behaviors that positively impacted the family and community. As the existence and influence of these institutions started to decrease in the 1960s, 1970s, and 1980s, social pressure on men and women to marry due to pregnancy also decreased. In the past, the social stigma of pre-marital births influenced the decision of many couples to marry. As time passed and cultural institutions weakened, marriage rates dropped. This drop was partly due to men no longer feeling obligated to marry for religious, social or cultural reasons.

A second factor contributing to the increase in father absence is the high rate of unemployment among African American males. The U.S. Census Bureau's American Community Survey reported data on the jobless rate of men, 20 to 33 years old, from 2010 to 2014, for 34 major cities. The data painted a very bleak reality for African American men. All the 34 major cities reported a black jobless rate above 45 percent. In these cities, most of the young black men were either jobless or imprisoned or unemployed. The age group studied in this survey represent men that are in the primary years of fathering children and having a family. A major factor contributing to the high rate of jobless men is partly due to the shift from producing industrial goods to low wage service jobs, innovations in technology, and the relocation of manufacturing jobs to suburban America. These changes in the economic landscape hurt African American men and their ability to provide for their families.

The loss of industrial jobs is a major factor in the increase of father absence. The rapid increase in unemployment had a significant impact on African American men and the ability to provide for their children. This caused a radical change in the family structure. Historically, African American men have been the head of the household and providers for their families. For African American men the family was a sanctuary from racial and economic oppression. However, as unemployment rates continued to rise, African American men struggled with the stress of providing for their families. Instead of the family being a sanctuary from racism and oppression, the family became a mirror that reflected his shortcomings as a man and father. In far too many families the mounting stress from a lack of finances produced feelings of anger, resentment, depression and substance abuse that ultimately tore the family apart.

In the 1970s and 1980s, blue-collar jobs began to disappear from the inner cities. Around the same time, women saw more opportunities to enter the workforce. Some women capitalized by getting college degrees and working white-collar jobs such as data entry/clerical, social work, health care, and other office jobs. As women became less reliant on men, they no longer felt a need to marry for financial reasons or the sake of their children. The social and cultural infrastructure that influenced couples to marry no longer had the power or influence of previous generations. Confident they could care for children on their own, single motherhood became an acceptable option for women. For those who did marry, getting a divorce was a socially acceptable way of ending a bad marriage. Today, more than half of all marriages end in divorce and eighty percent of all divorces are filed by women. In the best-case scenario, the couple works together to co-parent their children. In the worst-case scenario, divorce destroys the family and the father becomes absent from his child's life.

A third factor leading to the rise of absent fathers is the perpetuation of the family structure from one generation to the next. Studies have shown that children raised in father-absent homes are more likely to become single mothers or absent fathers. Some of the reasons given are a lack of adult guidance/supervision and living in impoverished neighborhoods where father absence is accepted as the norm. As a result, generations of African American boys are raised without a father figure to teach them how to be a man in a committed relationship. Without exposure to healthy men, the father-absent male struggles to learn the vital skills needed to be in committed relationships.

Relationship building skills are essential to maintaining a healthy family unit. Skills such as conflict resolution, anger management, and compromising help families stay together through difficult times. In homes where the mother is in a toxic relationship, the child misses the opportunity to learn important skills that empower families to stay together. Consequently, father-absent boys are at greater risk for engaging in behaviors that are counterproductive to healthy relationships because these skills were not part of his socialization or home environment.

Finally, the drug epidemic and mass incarceration during the 1980s and 1990s had a catastrophic effect on African American men and their families. The proliferation of crack cocaine devastated the African American community and the cultural institutions that supported them. Along with the explosion of crack cocaine was the loss of thousands of manufacturing jobs that allowed men to support their families. The loss of jobs combined with the availability of cheap drugs created the perfect storm to incarcerate millions of African American men. As drugs and violence increased in the black community, so did mass incarceration and the fragmentation of African American families.

According to an NAACP Criminal Justice Fact Sheet, between 1980 and 2015, the prison population increased from roughly 500,000 to over 2.2 million. Studies show that African Americans are incarcerated at more than five times the rate of whites. Additionally, African American women are incarcerated at twice the rate of white women and represent the fastest growing prison population in America. Behind the drive of mass incarceration is the privatization of prisons. Privatization made it necessary to have a consistent flow of African American men, women and teens to ensure profits for corporate investors. Consequently, when you look deeper into father absence you see a community under siege by drugs, mass incarceration and the decay of their social and economic infrastructure. All of these factors contributed to the rise of father absence in the African American community. The social institutions that supported African American families did not disappear on their own. They are the casualties of systemic racism and a predatory criminal justice system whose mission was to undermine the African American community for financial gain. Institutional and societal racism toward African American men and their families is well documented in American history. Even now some laws prohibit fathers from being in the home of their children if the mother is receiving government assistance. As a result, the African American family had to adapt and redefine itself to survive. For example, studies have shown the father-absent family is fluid and cannot be defined by the rigid boundaries of western society. In other words, a single female head of household does not mean a father is not involved in the lives of his children. Fathers who are absent from their children's home often, and still do play a significant role in their child's development.

A study conducted by Mott (1990) used data from the National Longitudinal Survey of Labor Market Experience of Youth (NLSY). Approximately 3,000 women and their children were surveyed periodically over four years. Mott's goal was to determine the "flow" of fathers in and out of the home and document the number "of never present fathers."

The results of the study showed that 8% of all non-black children had never lived with their biological father. Compared to 52% of the African American children who had never lived with their biological father. However, African American fathers who did not live in their child's home were much more likely to see their children frequently than their non-African American counterparts. The study concluded that even though African American men were not present in the home, they still spent time with their children. This is an indication that absent fathers are not all the same or fit the stereotype of deadbeat dads.

The researchers conducting the Mott study were unable to explain why African American fathers had more frequent contact with their children. One possible explanation is the ability of the African American community to redefine the concept of family and how its constructed. Instead of the family being defined through the narrow lens of western culture, the family is defined by the spiritual, cultural and emotional bonds that bring people together. This is not a new phenomenon. It is born from the need of people of African descent to cope with their traumatic history in the United States. For centuries the African American family was torn apart and sold into slavery. African American men, women and children endured unimaginable brutality as their families were terrorized and they struggled to stay together. Given the history of the black family in America, it was necessary to internalize a concept of family that was different from the typical narrow view used in Western culture.

It is not unusual for African Americans to live in an extended family that includes neighbors and family friends who became aunts and uncles to their children. This is consistent with the history and culture of people of African descent who were known to embrace people in their community as family. Embracing members of the community as part of the family was not only a strategy for survival. Adopting people into the family was also done to enrich the emotional and spiritual lives of the children as well. Therefore, it is important to note that African American families and fathers will not meet the narrow definitions typically used in Western culture. However, that does not mean they are deficient or dysfunctional. Their ability to adapt and redefine family should be viewed as a strength and not a weakness.

As stated in the opening of this chapter, the 1970s and 1980s saw African American female heads of households increase from thirty-three percent to fifty-five percent and the number continues to climb. However, when you look beyond the data you see a community and family structure under constant attack and struggling to survive. The loss of jobs, black-owned business and the declining influence of the Black Church left the family vulnerable to outside forces that sought to pull it apart. Consequently, father absence in the African American community is directly correlated to the destruction of its social/financial infrastructure, mass incarceration of black men, a proliferation of guns, drugs and the loss of jobs that occurred in the 1970s and 1980s and 1990s.

Chapter Two

The Impact of Poverty on the Father Absence Family

One major impact of father absence is the child and his family is more likely to live in poverty. Providing the basic human needs of food, clothing, and shelter is a struggle many single mothers face every day. The stress and frustration that comes from the day to day struggle of providing for a family have a major impact on the health of single mothers. Consequently, a study published in the American Journal of Public Health, reports that single mothers are 40% more likely to have cardiovascular health problems and 74% more likely to have a stroke compared to married mothers who work. They are also 77% more likely to smoke. Further complicating the lives of single moms is the stress of working low wage jobs that keep them in poverty and do not provide basic health benefits.

According to the 2014 Census Bureau American Community Survey study, 55% of all African American families with children are headed by a single mother. Forty-six percent of those families are living in poverty. This is compared to only 10% of married couples living below the poverty line. Even though 46% of African American female heads of households live in poverty, many have full-time minimum wage jobs that keep them trapped in poverty.

Studies have shown that a single mother of two needs to earn two and a half times the current minimum federal wage of $7.25 (about $18.00 per hr.) to sufficiently support her family. Without an income to realistically support a family, single mothers and their children are stuck in a cycle of poverty that's hard to escape. If we are ever going to address the plight of father-absent families, corporations and politicians must increase the minimum wage if single mothers are ever going to escape the cycle of poverty.

The socioeconomic status of a family has a significant impact on the overall wellbeing and health of father-absent boys. For the father-absent child, poverty is a factor from the time of conception throughout his entire life. For example, poor single mothers often do not have access to prenatal care during their pregnancy. As a result, infants born into poverty are at greater risk of being low birthweight babies and other chronic health problems.

Health problems continue to be an issue for poor children as they grow up. Children raised in poverty are at greater risk for malnutrition, asthma, obesity, diabetes, and other chronic conditions. Subjected to poverty and poor health the father-absent child can be physically, mentally and emotionally affected in ways that impact him socially and academically. Citing budget reasons, many schools have done away with breakfast programs and free meals. As a result, millions of children in poor neighborhoods are attending school and trying to learn on empty stomachs. Even with caring teachers doing their best to deal with budget cuts by bringing snacks to school, many students still sit in class hungry. This tragedy must be placed at the doorstep of politicians who cut food programs and corporations that have abandoned poor inner cities for suburban America and taking their tax dollars with them.

Further increasing the health risks for father-absent children is the lack of healthy foods in their communities. All too often poor families live in areas where it is hard to find affordable healthy fruits and vegetables. These neighborhoods are called "food deserts". For many single mothers finding fresh food means she must travel outside of her community to put a healthy meal on the table. Assuming she has transportation to travel out of her community, it's questionable that she can afford the cost of healthy food for her children.

On the other hand, highly processed fast foods and markets that sell low-quality products are abundant in neighborhoods where millions of father-absent boys are raised. These cheap, unhealthy, processed foods are often the staple diet of many inner-city children. Access to low cost, high-fat foods, packed with additives and preservatives is a factor in the rise of childhood obesity, diabetes and other health problems in the

African American community. Living in a community filled with unhealthy food choices makes it difficult to provide meals that prevent health problems instead of causing them. Sometimes a single mother is faced with choosing between feeding her children unhealthy food or not feeding them at all.

Another factor impacting families living in poverty is the amount of toxic waste in poor communities across America. Even though corporations abandoned the inner cities for suburban America, they did not take their toxic waste with them. The large factories that once provided jobs are now industrial ruins that pollute many inner-city neighborhoods. Exposure to dangerous levels of lead, benzene, methane and other chemicals are known to have a major impact on the health of children in poor communities across America.

The crisis of lead poisoning in Flint, Michigan is just one example of the devastating effects of toxic pollution in poor communities. Flint, Michigan was once part of a thriving major industrial region in the mid-west. Now, Flint is known for poisoning its citizens with deadly levels of lead in the drinking water. Flint Michigan is not the only city in the United States that is faced with dangerous environmental pollution. A 2009 article written in Forbes magazine titled America's Most Toxic Cities, identified Atlanta, Detroit, Houston, Chicago, Philadelphia, Cleveland, New York City and Los Angeles as some of the most toxic cities in the country.

All the cities reported in the Forbes article have large African American communities that are affected by toxins in their environment. As the Flint Michigan disaster continues to be studied, it can only be concluded that the political decisions were made with no regard for the health of people living in Flint. The effects of the Flint disaster and other toxic sites in urban areas will be felt for generations to come. Children and adults are already feeling the catastrophic impact of lead poisoning and other toxins in their environment. The decision of a few people in Flint has placed thousands of citizens at risk for birth defects, neurological disorders, cancer, and other chronic health problems. As is often the case, poor people of color will be disproportionately affected by the toxic waste that is polluting inner-city communities across the country. That means poor single mothers and their children.

Chapter Three

Parental Supervision Mental Health and Violence

Mental health, violence and the challenge of providing quality parental supervision are problems that significantly impact the lives of father-absent boys. In 1999, a document produced by the National Institute of Justice, titled, What Can the Federal Government Do to Decrease Crime in Revitalized Communities, reported the following statistics:

- Sixty-three percent of youth suicides are from father-absent homes.

- Ninety percent of all homeless and runaway youths are from father-absent homes.

- Eighty-five percent of children who exhibit behavioral disorders are from father-absent homes.

- Seventy-one percent of high school dropouts are from father-absent homes.

- Seventy percent of youth in State institutions come from father-absent families.

- Seventy-five percent of adolescent patients in substance abuse centers are father-absent children.

- Eighty-five percent of rapists motivated by displaced anger are raised in father-absent homes.

One factor that may contribute to statistics reported by the National Institute of Justice, is the lack of parental supervision in many father-absent homes. As mentioned earlier, many single mothers work long hours outside of the home. Consequently, it is a challenge to provide the supervision that many father-absent boys need. As a result, adolescent males are more likely to spend time out of their homes with other teens who also lack adult supervision. Inner-city youth who do not have structure and supervision have been shown to have more involvement with street gangs than teens from two-parent homes. This may account for why 70% of juveniles in State-operated facilities come from father-absent homes (Statistics on Fatherless Children in America). Working long hours on low paying jobs leaves little time for parental supervision and structured family activities. Without a support network, father-absent boys are often raised without the benefit of a structured environment to ensure their wellbeing and safety.

Children from father-absent homes are more likely to struggle with depression, bullying, suicidal thoughts, and posttraumatic stress from exposure to violence. The statistics reported by the National Institute of Justice suggests there is a mental health crisis in father-absent families. A lack of mental health care and school-based programs further exacerbates the crisis. Even though single mothers are trying to perform the herculean task of raising an adolescent son without a father. The data suggests far too many mothers are losing the battle.

Growing up in high crime areas can desensitize children to violence. It can cause feelings of distrust, anger, and anxiety, particularly around strangers. Children exposed to violence at an early age are also at risk for developing a "hostile bias," which influences how they perceive and react to people. Children that have a hostile bias often interpret unfamiliar people or situations as threatening or an act of aggression. A study conducted by Courtney and Cohen (1996), found that children exposed to violence process things differently from those that are not exposed to violence. Their study reported that in ambiguous situations children with a hostile bias used fewer cues, made more hostile interpretations of the other child's intent and generated a higher percentage of aggressive responses.

Exposure to violence can teach a child that using aggression is an acceptable way of solving problems. Children who grow up with a hostile bias often subscribe to what is called the "code of the streets." The code dictates that respect must be earned at all costs, even if it means resorting to violence. This "street code," places a high value on using physical strength or violence to resolve conflict and gain power. Adolescent males viewed as the strongest receive the most respect and those viewed as weak learn to stay in their place. The street code establishes a social order with clear rules of engagement between stronger and weaker males. Breaking the rules is viewed as a sign of disrespect and violence is used to re-establish order within the group.

Children are shaped by their experiences and environment. But African American males, particularly those in inner cities are believed to be innately or genetically predisposed to being violent. They are not! All children regardless of ethnicity who are exposed to violence are more likely to engage in aggressive behavior to resolve conflict. Violence is a learned behavior. Conversely, if violence is a learned behavior, then non-violent behavior can be learned as well. For many adolescents growing up in New York, Chicago, Detroit, and other urban cities, the use of violence is seen as necessary for survival. However, when the same youth are given options, positive role models and taught conflict resolution skills there is a reduction in violent behavior. African American students, particularly father-absent boys, do not need the harsh punishment (immediate suspension and expulsion) many schools have adopted. What's needed are more in school programs and social skills training at an early age. Additionally, the school system should hire more African

American men to work in inner-city schools. A July 2017 USA Today article reported that only 2% of the teachers in the public-school system are African American men. Studies have shown that exposing male students to healthy role models increases their academic performance and decreases in-school violence.

Schools that invest in their students and teachers see improvements in academic performance and a reduction in school violence. For example, West Side High School, in Newark, New Jersey, had a problem where students were being bullied and targeted on social media. The principal, Mr. Akbar Cook discovered that the students were targeted because their clothes were dirty, and they often had a body order when came to school. To avoid being bullied some students chose not to come to school. The principal solved the problem by building a laundry mat on the school premises. The students are now able to wash their clothes for free and the bullying of the students stopped. This is an example of a commonsense solution that empowered students and created a positive peer culture at the school. Instead of perpetuating the stereo typical images of poor African American males as violent criminals. Why not invest in programs we know will work such as performance arts/music, sports, and after school programs? Why are young African American males demonized as the most violent men in America? Do these images exist because they serve an important purpose in American society? The answer is 'yes.'

Images of violent males have been used to elect politicians, create a police state in poor communities and produce fear in suburban America. Irrational fear was the motivation used by corporate America to abandon urban areas for the suburbs. This had a devastating effect on African American families. It also caused the deterioration of the economic and social infrastructure of urban cities. Community schools, small businesses, and black owned banks were all hurt by the loss of jobs in urban America. Inner cities in the United States were reported to be war zones that could not be tolerated by corporate America. As a result, white flight created jobs in the suburbs and the criminalization of African American males was turned into big business.

According to Wikipedia, statistics from the U.S. Department of Justice report, as of 2013, there were 133,000 state and federal prisoners housed in privately owned prisons in the U.S., constituting 8.4% of the overall U.S. prison population. African Americans and Latinos make up most of the inmates held in private prisons. Today, prisons are a multi-billion-dollar industry supported by criminalizing African Americans males and other people of color for corporate profit.

Father absence boys are the raw material used by a billion dollar industry to create wealth for an elite class of people in America. This elite class shapes the narrative that is used to criminalize people of color. It has existed for centuries and has destroyed countless black lives and families. The most powerful (government/private) institutions in America help to create the conditions that perpetuate father absence in black families. For example, instead of investing in economic development and schools, private prisons were built. And stereotypical images of violent African American males were used to justify building the prisons. Building prisons meant there had to be a pipeline to ensure they would be full and profitable. The educational system fulfilled the need for the prison pipeline. Generations later, millions of black children are counted on to fill prisons and make predatory corporations rich.

The education system manages the classroom to prison pipeline by maintaining close to two thousand schools known as "dropout factories." These are schools where less than 60% of freshmen reach their senior year and graduate. They produce a steady flow of young bodies (mostly poor African American males) for the prison system. When the dropout factories have done their job, the criminal justice system ensures that privately owned prisons are full and profitable. One example of how this system works is known as the "kids for cash" scandal. In 2011, a former juvenile court judge in Pennsylvania, Mark Ciavarella Jr., was sentenced to 28 years for accepting kickbacks and unjustly sending children to privately run detention centers. Judge Ciavarella Jr., was part of a larger political system that creates the illusion of democracy, while it enforces laws and policies to preserve power for an elite group of people. Finally, the monetary system, which controls the banks, interest rates and the flow of capital, makes sure money stays in the hands of the rich and not the poor. If you want to understand generational poverty and father absence in the black community, you must examine who profits from these social conditions.

It's important to examine the systems that maintain the status quo of wealth, poverty and violence that impacts the lives of father-absent families. When you do, it's clear the power structure defines who is a criminal and who is not while they profit from those decisions. History shows poor people of color are identified as criminals. Particularly African American men and boys. Meanwhile, those who maintain a system unjust are not seen as criminals. Consequently, when studies are done, they typically look at black on black crime. They ignore white collar and institutional crimes committed against the black community.

Institutional crime affects the lives of millions of people and it should be understood as acts of violence against the black community. These acts of violence contribute to illness, premature death and the victimization of people of color. For example, as mentioned in the previous chapter, the poisoning of Flint, Michigan's water system impacted the lives of thousands of people. However, the politicians and corporations that caused the disaster were not viewed as criminals. To date, only one employee in Flint, Michigan has been convicted of a crime. Additionally, the toxic waste poisoning our cities is not viewed as an act of violence against poor people in urban America. While the white-collar crimes are committed, it's the African American male who is portrayed as the poster child for crime and violence in America. Meanwhile, the CEO's of some of the largest companies in the world are not considered criminals, even though their actions caused the illness and death of millions of people.

Another example of how systems of power criminalize one community and not another is their response to the opioid crisis. Opioid addiction has mainly been confined to suburban America. Thousands of lives and families have been destroyed by the drug epidemic. Meanwhile, the pharmaceutical companies responsible for flooding the country with drugs have gone unpunished by the political and criminal justice system. Even though, some physicians have been convicted for overprescribing opioids. The corporations and their CEO's who made billions of dollars have not been charged with a crime. Why? Because it's the elite who shape the narrative that decides who the criminals are in America.

And what was the response of politicians to the opioid crisis? They declared the opioid crisis a national health problem and allocated billions of dollars for drug and mental health treatment. Their response is a stark contrast to the crack epidemic in the 1980s and 1990s. Both crises destroyed millions of families in suburban and black communities. However, suburban America received the mental health and drug treatment they needed to keep their families intact. Meanwhile, the response to the crisis in the black community was mass incarceration and more prisons. When you examine mental health, violence, and crime in urban communities, it's clear that services to heal father-absent families are not a priority. It appears the priority is to maintain the conditions that perpetuate poverty and the father-absent family.

Chapter Four

Father Absence Impact on Adolescent Identity and Self-Concept

Adolescence is a challenging time for young people. It is a time when they are seeking autonomy from their parents and want to gain acceptance from their peers. Their bodies are going through physical changes as they try to figure out their place in the world. Adolescence is also when young people want to know about their family history, their culture and how to deal with the physical changes to their bodies. Asking questions such as, "who am I, and how do I fit in this world," is part of the process of adolescent identity development.

Father-absent boys who struggle to find answers to life's critical questions can experience identity issues that impact them in their adult years. It can leave a child feeling rejected by his father, causing him to question himself and his mother. Consequently, they may experience the absence of their father as being unworthy of his love. This negative perception can have a significant impact on a child's identity. Internalized paternal rejection can result in feelings of inadequacy, depression, and anger toward himself, his mother, and his absent father. If he is unable to express his anger, he may engage in acting out behaviors as a cry for help. Without the proper guidance to cope with his emotions, the father-absent child can internalize his anger, become withdrawn, anxious and depressed.

One way boys cope with father absence is to internalize an idealized image of their father as a part of their identity. In this case, the father has a larger than life image which leaves the adolescent feeling he can never be as good as his father. Conversely, the adolescent may be inclined to develop a negative image of his father as well. In this case, he fosters the belief that he is worthless like his father. This is particularly true if the child has grown up in an environment hearing negative messages about his father. A distorted image, whether positive or negative, places the adolescent in a no-win situation and can cause him to feel angry and confused.

It's natural for a child to have questions about his biological family of origin. Identity is important because it's how the adolescent views himself, his family and community. In a family where both parents, grandparents and other elders are present, the adolescent can see a broader picture of his family's history and legacy. The presence of his father creates a balance between masculine and feminine energy in the child's life. As he reaches adolescence and questions "who am I," the adolescent looks to his father, instead of outside influences for answers. The adolescent sees characteristics in his father he identifies with or chooses to disassociate from. He watches his father to see if he is a man of integrity, a protector and provider for his family. Does his father respect women? Is he affectionate to his child, wife or the mother of his children? What he sees lays the foundation for his identity. The child's identity becomes an extension of what he sees in the home with his father and mother. It also determines how he defines masculinity and manhood as well.

Father-absent boys like all boys need masculine energy and attention. His desire to be in the presence of men, particularly his father is essential to male identity development. Boys look to their fathers for guidance, knowledge, and skills that empower them to thrive in their environment. As he enters adolescence his mind and body are going through massive changes. No longer a child, he is perceived differently by his mother, siblings, family members and people in his environment. As he matures expectations change and he must learn to be responsible for his behavior. He is no longer a small non-threatening child. The adolescent is now an African American male with physical size and strength. For some people, the size and presence of an African American male can be intimidating and viewed as a threat. So, boys need to understand the changes they undergo during adolescence and how those changes are perceived by people around them.

When father-absent boys are exposed to healthy masculine energy they learn when, where and how to use their strength. For example, a positive role model teaches the father-absent boy that violence against girls is unacceptable. He observes how a mature man respects, communicates and resolves conflicts with women. Seeing a man relate positively to women sets an example for the father-absent child to be respectful, and control his anger, particularly with women and girls. This standard of behavior is internalized as part of the adolescent's identity. It also builds the character and confidence not to succumb to peer pressure and other negative influences in the community.

When the father or positive male role model is not present there can be a significant void in the child's life. Even though, he might not understand why he profoundly feels the absence of his father. If the need for masculine energy/attention is not met, it can lead to behavioral and emotional problems beginning in early childhood. If his anger is not channeled properly, behavior problems can occur in the home or school, as he struggles to cope with feelings he does not understand. In some cases, the mother becomes the object of the boy's anger, as he blames her for his father's absence. In other cases, the boy's anger is directed at his absent father, who he blames for abandoning his mother. In either scenario, he experiences complex emotions that shape his identity as a child and a man.

When the father-absent child has unanswered questions about his mother or father, he can feel lonely and confused. On one hand, he feels a deep connection and desire to protect his mother. But he questions why his father is not in his life. Is it because of his mother? Did she make a mistake in her choice of men? Did his father leave because his mother is somehow flawed or not a good woman? Is his father a "loser" if so, then why did she choose him? Like a person feeling his way around a dark room, the father-absent child wants to escape from the confusion and find answers to his questions. Not knowing the answers to these questions only fuels his frustration and anger. With proper guidance, he can work through his anger and frustration. Without proper guidance, he is subject to adopting a toxic identity. One that is hyper-masculine, angry and uses aggression to resolve conflict. When this happens, it can have a profound impact on his mother and other family members.

The absence of a father is not only felt by the child. It is felt by the mother as well. It leaves a void that only a woman can understand. She is vulnerable to the effects of not having a committed partner to help raise her child. Single mothers and their children are among the poorest in the United States. Consequently, the effects of poverty and lack of adult supervision are residual effects of father absence. In some cases, the mother out of her need for masculine energy raises her son to be the man of the house. This is a burden that should not be placed on the shoulders of any boy. If he is the man of the house why does he have to listen to his mother, teachers, and other authority figures? Or, as the "man" is he free to do what he wants in his house? This is a paradoxical situation that cannot be resolved in the mind of a child. How can a child assume a role he is not mentally, emotionally or physically prepared for? Unable to meet his mother's expectation, he is left feeling angry and confused. As a result, the father-absent child is in a no-win situation that can set him up for failure.

The father-absent adolescent's search for identity is often an emotionally driven and confusing process. Not seeing a reflection of himself in the home, he looks outward to media figures, celebrities and males in his community to define manhood. He establishes bonds with teenage boys who are also from father-absent homes. The anger and confusion he dealt with in isolation, is now affirmed by his peers, as they struggle together with the same issues of father absence and identity. Father-absent boys who grow up in large urban cities without a positive role model are often overexposed to negative images of black men and hyper-masculinity. These images associate masculinity with physical strength, violence, and aggression. Materialism is valued over spiritualism. Competition is valued more than cooperation. Emotional detachment is seen as a strength and showing emotions, other than anger is viewed as a weakness. As a result, the adolescent's identity is a misguided process that lacks the guidance of a father or other positive role model.

Unfortunately, struggling with identity, unresolved anger and issues of manhood is a problem millions of father-absent males must overcome. There are reports as high as 73% of the households in the African American community being father-absent homes. As a result, millions of African American children are growing up in poverty. They are raised in homes where the mother is overworked and unable to spend quality time with her son. Unable to supervise her son, he is vulnerable to adopting the values he learns from his peers and the big city streets. This sets him up for poor academic performance, gang affiliation, incarceration and other dangers of the streets.

When you examine the identity of millions of African American males in urban America, you see an identity that is prescribed to him by society. The identity did not evolve from seeing a man in the home who was committed to his wellbeing. The identity is not a product of the rich history and legacy of African and African American people. The identity adopted by many males evolved from the racist stereotypes rooted in American culture. It's an identity that is hyper-masculine, impulsive, emotionally constricted and uses violence to resolve conflicts. It does not prepare him to be a loving husband or father. The image of hyper-masculinity is the antithesis of a loving man, husband, and father. The hyper-masculine identity adopted by many young black men inhibits their ability to commit to a woman and the children he fathers. Having sex and not taking responsibility for his child becomes the misguided measure of manhood he learned from the streets. Consequently, the boy who grew up knowing the pain of father absence perpetuates the family structure by becoming an absent father himself.

Chapter Five

The Effect of Father Absence on
High School Completion

In the United States, 1.2 million students drop out of school every year. The U.S. ranks 22nd out of 27 developed countries in high school dropout rates. According to the U.S. Department of Education (Fast Facts-Dropout) statistics, 71% of dropouts are from father-absent homes and high school dropouts commit 75% of the crimes in the U.S. These statistics paint a bleak picture of public education in urban America. The picture tells a story. It says, 'the classroom to prison pipeline is fully functional. It is a highly efficient system producing a steady flow of young black males for the prison population.

Public education in the United States is big business. According to the National Center for Education Statistics, 50 million students attended public schools in 2018. That represents billions of taxpayers' dollars. However, the children who are the poorest, with the greatest need for resources, do not receive the help they need to be successful. This is supported by an article written in the New York Times (Feb. 27, 2019), that states, "school districts that predominantly serve students of color received $23 billion less in funding than mostly white school districts in the United States in 2016 despite serving the same number of students." Poor children usually attend one of the two thousand schools throughout the United States known as "dropout factories." More than two million students attend these schools. They are primarily located in poor urban cities and produce more than half of the dropouts in the United States. Crippled by a lack of resources, training, and young teachers unprepared to address the challenges of their students, dropout factories maintain a culture of low expectation and academic failure.

With the odds stacked against them, father-absent boys in poor neighborhoods start falling behind soon after entering school. Attending mostly overcrowded schools with a high teacher-student ratio, they often do not receive the individualized attention needed to learn basic skills in reading, math, and English. Without support, the father-absent child falls further behind with each grade. Unable to keep up he is often identified as, "learning disabled." This label comes with a social stigma that can diminish the child's ability to learn and his self-esteem. Consequently, they are put on an educational tract that often leads to dropping out of school and into the prison pipeline.

Another systemic factor contributing to the high dropout rate is the zero-tolerance policy adopted by many schools in poor neighborhoods. To deal with school violence, administrators are quick to expel students without explanation. Suspensions can be automatic even for small infractions, particularly for students of color and those identified as learning disabled. Interventions such as in-school suspension and after school detention are a thing of the past. Unfortunately, expulsion and suspension are like an educational death sentence that leaves students locked out of school with few alternatives to the streets. Many of the expelled students end up involved in gangs, drugs, crime or prison. This is supported by the data which reports that seventy percent of adolescents in juvenile detention are from father-absent homes.

When you examine the impact of father absence on high school graduation, its clear poverty affects every area of the child's life. A study done by Mulkey, Craine, and Herrington suggests that single parenting can negatively affect African American boys graduating from high school. They report that father-absent children are less closely supervised and have more school-related negative behaviors. The variables used to best explain why father absence lowers student's grades are: student absenteeism, lateness, not doing homework, and recurrent behavioral problems in the classroom.

There are several contributing factors to the father-absent adolescent's low graduation rate. First, as mentioned in the previous chapter, adolescents from father-absent homes are less likely to receive adult supervision and guidance. Being time-poor is a major factor for single mothers. Adolescents lacking adequate adult supervision are more likely to spend time out of the home. Consequently, they can be vulnerable to negative influences in the streets and peer pressure. An unsupervised adolescent is more likely to engage in unmonitored social activities, leaving less time for studying, completing homework assignments and getting adequate rest for school.

Secondly, father-absent boys are more likely to be raised by a single mother who did not graduate from high school. Studies suggest that a parent's level of education is an important factor when examining high school completion rates. One study conducted by Manski, Sandefur, McLanahan, and Powers used data from the National Longitudinal Study of Youth to investigate the effect of family structure on high school graduation. Results indicated a parent's level of education contributes substantially to a child's success in school. The study concluded that a child's graduation from high school increased significantly with a parent's education regardless of the family structure. The study also examined the educational level of dual parent households and single-parent households. It concluded that it is the parent's education and not the family structure that increases the probability of high school graduation.

Parents with lower levels of education may be unaware or unable to provide an enriching environment that mentally stimulates their child. Educational materials in the home such as personal computers, laptops, books, and access to the internet are costly but essential tools for academic success. Having the right tools for learning enriches the student's home environment and conveys the importance of education to the child. The adolescent living in a family without the essential tools or doesn't value education will have a hard time keeping up in school.

The studies discussed in this chapter are a clear indication that educational resources, training, and support are critical for single mothers. Improving educational outcomes for young single mothers not only improves their standard of living, but it also improves the child's school performance as well. Effective strategies to improve the quality of life for single mothers must be a priority if we are serious about addressing the dropout rates for father absence boys. Providing support to single mothers improves the chances of father-absent boys completing high school and staying out of the classroom to prison pipeline.

When you look at the disproportionate rate of failure for poor students of color it's important to recognize that a system with fifty million students will never meet the needs of its most vulnerable students. It was not created to meet the educational needs of African American children. Public education from the beginning was created to produce a product and student who works for the best interest of the elite in America. It has done that for generations. Over the generations, it has grown into an institutional system with fifty million students. Based on the data at least one million of those students will drop out and potentially end up in the prison system.

On the surface, it appears the public education system is a failure. It is not! In suburban and small-town America, it is not failing. In urban cities where there has been an influx of middleclass whites who change the community, the schools are not failing. Those parts of the system have expectations of graduating their students. These students will assume their place in middle-class America. Some of them will go on to college, others will work various jobs, but they will ultimately serve the interest of the wealthy and elite. It also appears the educational system is a failure for African Americans who attend poorly funded schools known as "dropout factories." It is not! This part of the system expects its students to drop out by creating the conditions for failure. These students are expected to stay poor, produce father-absent children and maintain a steady flow of African American males to the prison population. When you understand the purpose of public education it becomes clear that it is succeeding at maintaining the status quo of wealth, poverty and father absence in America.

Public education was not created to empower the minds of young African American boys and girls. It also was not created to free the minds of the masses of white students. Its purpose is to maintain the status quo of elitism by perpetuating the illusion of superiority of one race over the other. This allows an elite group of people to reap the benefits of racial division. As a result, neither black or white students come out of the system free of the bias and prejudice that fuels racial tension in America. The system was never designed to educate 50 million students, particularly poor inner-city students from father-absent homes.

However, it was designed to serve the best interest of the elite and it continues to serve that purpose today. That's why two thousand "dropout factories" exist primarily in cities with large populations of brown and black people. Their purpose is to produce failing students who will be poor, incarcerated and absent from the lives of their children. According to the data, the educational system is very successful when it comes to failing brown and black people.

The federal education budget is approximately sixty billion dollars. Individual States and cities add billions more in funding to the education budget. Yet generations of father-absent boys continue to attend failing schools in dilapidated buildings. Adding to the dysfunction are decisions of politicians who allocate resources but do not represent the communities most affected by their policies. Their decisions impact teachers who often want to make a difference in the lives of their students, but they lack the resources. Consequently, every year more students fall behind and eventually drop out because they don't have the resources and support, they need to succeed. Many of them will become young parents and continue the cycle of family poverty.

Chapter Six

Looking Deeper to the Cause of
Father Absence

Despite enormous sums of money spent by government and social agencies, the number of father-absent homes continues to rise. The research on father-absent children reports that they are among the poorest and have some of the worse outcomes in education, incarceration, and health. Even though the poor outcomes are well documented, father-absent families and particularly African American boys, are less likely to receive the support they need in times of distress.

There are two thousand schools in the United States known as "dropout factories". Most of them are in large urban cities. They are entrusted with the most vulnerable members of our community, our children. For decades the system has miseducated and failed to provide support for the poorest children in their care. Whether the need is for academic support, counseling or medical treatment, studies have shown the safety net is not there for black students when compared to white students. This is particularly true for African American males who are expelled and identified as "learning disabled", more often when compared to their white counterparts.

The educational system and social agencies that study father-absent families use language like "inappropriate behavior, hyperactive, aggressive, learning disabled and anti-social," to describe African American boys. Researchers identify "red flags," such as anxiety, depression and developmental issues that impact a child's ability to learn. However, the recognition of red flags has not translated into educational, medical or mental health services for African American children in need. Studies have shown poor children of color are least likely to receive counseling, they are more likely to be misdiagnosed and do not receive treatment when they have contact with health care providers.

The treatment community identifies racial bias and ineffective communication as barriers to assessing and treating African American children. The barriers to treatment are not new to health care providers. The reported obstacles to treatment have been there for decades. What is missing is the ethical and moral will power to remove the barriers to treatment. Meanwhile, children of color are misdiagnosed and do not receive the care they need. And students who attend "dropout factories", are funneled into the classroom to prison pipeline. This has gone on for generations in the black community. Yet there seems to be a lack of understanding of the causes of father absence. Given the data reported about "dropout factories', it is easy to conclude they are designed to fail children of color. When it comes to education these schools are highly effective at feeding father-absent boys into the prison system. And that is why they continue to exist. Consequently, when you look deeper into the root cause of father absence you see systems of power whose purpose is to create the conditions that fragment the black family and community.

The lack of treatment and support from public education and health care is partly due to focusing on describing the problem and not looking at the root cause of father absence. Government agencies talk about high school dropout rates, poverty, violence, and crime. However, researchers do not talk about the proliferation of drugs that flow in some communities and not others. Studies do not talk about how discriminatory banking and corporate flight are root causes for much of the poverty that has fragmented black families. To understand how and why father absence exists, researchers must move beyond describing the outcomes and look at the systemic causes of father absence. Otherwise, it appears father absence is a social condition that is limited to African American men. To come to such a conclusion, a person would have to be blind to the effects of institutional racism and four hundred years of American history.

The studies conducted by government and social agencies only look at the symptoms and not the underlying cause of father absence. To understand the father-absent problem, you must look deeper than the political and social interpretations of outcome data. Otherwise, you will be led to believe African American men, women and children are incapable of loving families. A deeper look into the interpretations and conclusions of research provides insight into how institutions think about the people they study. When the subject is black men, you see a narrative that is rooted in stereotypes, bias, and racism. The narrative contributes to the language that sets the agenda for how black men will be perceived and treated in America. Like a computer using technical language to program its operation. The interpretations of research and data contribute to the narrative that dictates who receives services and who does not.

If research is used to justify the allocation of resources to those who need it the most. Then why are children of color last to receive services when the data suggests they have the greatest need? It's because the outcome data is only part of the story. What is most important are the decisions/actions of the people using the data. Just because millions of dollars are spent studying children of color, does not mean the information will be used to provide services to those in need. Historically, the information collected on people of color has been used to justify closing health care centers, building prisons, over- policing, ending breakfast programs, closing afterschool centers and other destructive policies. When you look at the root of father absence you see well thought out policies by government and corporations to maintain a segment of the African American population in a state of chaos and generational poverty. There is a fear of African American men, woman and families coming together to act in their own best interest. A unified family and community represent trillions of dollars in spending and that is a power that must be controlled. Consequently, the head of the family must remain weakened, unable to provide or protect his family.

The narrative used by government agencies to isolate, incarcerate and mis-educate black males paint him as a threat to society. Science and research are used to justify the narrative. As a result, black men are portrayed in the media as uncaring and unloving fathers. While those who create the conditions for father absence go undetected and reap billions of dollars from the pain of black men and the fragmentation of their families.

Beyond the biased narrative used to attack black males are men who continue to fight for their family and community. Like everyone else, African American men want to protect and provide for their children. The poorest members of our community remain in poverty not because they choose to. They stay in poverty because when it is time to provide support and resources they are denied based on the color of their skin. Children of color, particularly poor father-absent boys are viewed as expendable. Their value comes only from being a commodity for the multi-billion-dollar social service industry that provides jobs for mostly white lower- and middle-class citizens. If African Americans disappeared from the criminal justice system and other government/private agencies, millions of people would lose their jobs. The system is dependent on masses of poor people of color to support the economy and justify the existence of failing government agencies.

If you want to understand the cause and effect of father absence you must look at how the systems of power carry out their mission. In the African American community systems of power are created to function the exact opposite of their stated mission and purpose. For example, the criminal justice system was not created to ensure justice for African Americans. It does the exact opposite. Instead of ensuring justice, the system ensures the interest of a small elite group is protected while filling prisons with poor white, brown and black people, particularly African American males. They do it for profit and to maintain a permanent underclass in America. All institutions of control and power function the same way, including the educational system. It does this by maintaining inferior schools, mis-educating children of color and distorting their true history. If you look at the name and title of American institutions (justice, banking, political, etc.), you will see their function is the opposite of their title in the African American community. All the institutions of control and power act in the best interest of the elite and to the detriment of people of color.

African American families have fought injustice, predatory lending, inferior public schools and the misuse of political power for centuries. The role government agencies play in fragmenting the family is an indication they will not and cannot generate effective solutions to father absence. If black families are going to heal, the solutions must come from the African American community. Culturally conscious men and women are the only ones who can generate lasting solutions for African American families. Father-absent boys are thirsty for positive masculine energy and attention that only African American men can give them.

To be part of the solution men must do the work necessary to heal spiritually, mentally and emotionally. That means reaching out for counseling, coaching, and elders in their communities to get the information, support and help needed to heal. We must create opportunities and networks where men and boys can connect, communicate, collaborate and heal. Healing is not necessary because African American men are inferior or deficient. No! Healing is needed because of the persistent assault on African American men and their families. The social narrative in America says black men are an expendable commodity. The system is programmed to accept the collateral damage of black lives without consciousness or remorse. Sadly, the acceptable level of collateral damage has risen to the count of millions of black lives. When you look at father-absent families you see a perpetual cycle of poverty that is destroying the hopes and dreams of black children. Men and women of color must come together and realize they are the only ones who can resolve the issues confronting the black family. If African American men and women do not look to one another for healing and strength, the family as we know it will not survive.

The survival of the family begins and ends with African American men and women. The notion that black men and women can survive and thrive without each other discards a million years of human history. The devastating effects of father absence discussed in this book is evidence that black men are essential to saving the family. No family structure, human or animal can survive if the male and female do not work together to secure a future for the next generation. The critical question we must ask ourselves is, do we as a people accept the narrative that poor black men, women, and children are an expendable commodity in America? If the answer is "yes", then you are part of the problem and not the solution.

Chapter Seven

Healing and Bridging the Gap between African American Men and Boys

Father absence inflicts wounds that can last a lifetime. For many boys, the question "why did my father leave me", is one that haunts him well into adulthood. Even with a loving mother, emotional scars can take a lifetime to heal. When the wounds are deep and unresolved, father-absent males can develop trust issues that make it difficult to be in a committed relationship, even with their children. At an early age, the father-absent child can learn to fear being close to someone that can cause him emotional pain. So, he copes with his fear by guarding his emotions and staying in a comfort zone to protect his feelings

Growing up with unanswered questions and fear, the father-absent child can build a wall to maintain emotional distance. This allows him to avoid risking the pain of rejection he felt from his father. Consequently, in adulthood, many father-absent males become comfortable with superficial relationships to avoid meaningful connections. Without the lessons that come from being committed he learns to walk away from relationships to distance himself from the pain he feels and causes. As a result, the effects of father absence can impact him throughout his lifetime. If unresolved, the father-absent male is at risk of never learning the social skills to be in a healthy relationship. That includes relationships with women and his children.

The father-absent male's fear of rejection can impact his ability to build trusting relationships with people, particularly women. Therefore, they must receive the help they need to overcome the impact of father absence. Teaching boys how to work through their trust and abandonment issues facilitates healing. Without help, studies show that father-absent males are at greater risk of fathering multiple children and perpetuating the single mother household. Thereby, continuing the cycle of poverty and father absence from one generation to the next. As a psychologist and consultant, I have worked with males from all walks of life, including college campuses, juvenile detention facilities, jails, and prisons. Many of them grew up in father-absent homes. For the most part, they all wanted a better life and recognized the need for more education and skills. Most of the young men also wanted someone in their life they can trust, someone who will teach them about manhood and fatherhood as well.

Even though most of the males I've worked with wanted a better life, there was a small number who did not want to turn their lives around. They were stuck in their pain and determined to live by their own rules no matter how many people they hurt. For example, in a workshop, I was conducting at a correctional facility a young male proudly talked about his father having twenty children. All from different women. He was 26 years old. He knew who his father was, but the man spent most of his life in and out of prison, so he never had contact with him. He also met three of his siblings but never had a chance to meet the other sixteen children conceived by his father. At the age of 26, this young man already had eight children and a pregnant woman waiting for him to come home. When asked if he wanted more children he said, "yes, I want as many as my father." After attending several workshops, he talked about the anger and pain he felt growing up as a child. He couldn't understand why his father never came to see him or took care of him. He learned to cope with his pain by creating a fantasized image of his father and consciously or unconsciously decided to be like him. Over time, he shut his emotions down and replaced them with the façade of being unaffected by his pain. Like his father, he spent most of his life in and out of prison and did not have a relationship with his children or the women who gave birth to them.

This 26-year-old male was afraid of emotional connections and the responsibilities that came with them. As a result, he learned to be detached from his actions and the responsibility of fathering eight children. As we talked and other men shared similar experiences you could see the young man become aware of the pain he caused and years of bottled up emotions started pouring out. When men open up and talk about the pain of father absence the healing that can take place is miraculous. I don't know what his life will be like when he is released from prison. But if untreated, it is frightening to think of the pain this 26-year-old will cause in the lives of women and children. How many generations of father-absent children will he be responsible for creating in the African American community?

For some people, the thought of a twenty-six-year-old having eight children sounds like an extreme case. I would agree it is extreme, but it is not unheard of in some communities. I have worked with many young males who fathered multiple children and they were still in their twenties. Despite the pain of growing up without a father, it did not end the cycle of father absence in their families. The man in my workshop grew up and never received the help he needed to heal his anger and pain. He went through life masking his anger. For him, fathering children was a demonstration of his manhood. It's frightening to know that he is only one of the millions of black children who never heal from the pain of father absence.

When we talk about addressing the problems of father absence, it is important to note that we are not talking about most men in the African American community. Just like any other race, African American men love and want the best for their children. However, it does not take an army of unconscious males to impact a community by fathering multiple children. If 10 teenage boys father 3 children each, that's 30 children in one urban neighborhood. That means a new generation of 30 children will potentially grow up in a home without a father. As a result, these children are more likely to live in poverty, drop out of high school and create father-absent families as well. This is how a small number of males can devastate communities for generations to come. The idea of ten males fathering multiple children in a single neighborhood is not farfetched.

Unfortunately, it is a reality in every major city in America. Throughout urban America, there are a minority of unconscious males wreaking havoc on an already vulnerable community. They do not represent most African American men who work every day to take care of their children. Yet, the staggering number of father-absent children is a reality in poor neighborhoods across America. As a result, it is critical that unconscious males who inflict the most damage be identified in the community. Some effort must be made to help them see the damage they are causing. If we can reach the males who are creating father-absent families, we can change the lives of generations of children.

The increase in father-absent homes cannot and will not be solved by government programs. Even African American women with all their love cannot give their sons everything they need to become men. Only African American men can give them the masculine energy and attention they hunger for. It's easy to think father absence is a problem too big to solve. It is a huge problem affecting millions of children, but we must start somewhere. We are not striving for perfection. We are striving to make progress and help the most vulnerable members of our community, poor women and children. A mass movement is not needed, nor will it be effective. What is needed are committed men working together to touch the lives of boys in their neighborhoods. Improving the lives of a small number of boys in a community can impact a family for generations to come. Just ending the cycle of father absence in one family will uplift a generation of children. Conscious men must initiate the healing process and guide father-absent boys through the process of becoming men. Why? Because only African American men possess the blueprint for being a strong black man in America. Men must reach out and teach young boys how to survive and thrive despite their experience of father absence.

When the gap between young and old is bridged it's clear that African American boys are open to the wisdom and knowledge that can improve their lives. Their minds and hearts are receptive to men who honestly want to help them succeed in life. If a few unconscious males can devastate a community. It is also possible a few culturally conscious men can transform a community as well. Government agencies will not and cannot effectively address the problem. They can play a role by providing resources and access to the thousands of men in prison and the children trapped in schools known as "dropout factories". People of color are the only ones that can end father absence in their community. It starts with black men assuming the lead role in reclaiming the minds, bodies, and spirits of their children.

Chapter Eight

Can Cultural Identity Protect Father-Absent Boys and their Families?

The steady increase in father-absent families poses a serious threat to the wellbeing of millions of African American men, women and children. If we do not take it upon ourselves to create and build a safety net to uplift the most vulnerable members of our community, the African American family as we know it will cease to exist. Work must be done to rebuild a social infrastructure to counteract the systems of power such as, the classroom to prison pipeline and dropout factories that miseducate millions of children and prepare them for incarceration.

The assault on African American men and their families has persisted for hundreds of years. People of color around the world are growing weary of battling an enemy who believes he is superior to everyone else, even to the planet earth. Given our history, there is no reason to believe the assault on black people will stop. It will not! The assault on people of color is blind to your financial status and educational level. Even affluent communities like the one in California, where Lebron James lives was targeted with the words "go home nigger", spray painted on his mansion. The intent of the message was clear. And some poor white person did not travel to this affluent neighborhood to spray paint his house. The message was written by someone who comes from wealth and probably lives in the community. The intent was to spread fear and send a message that "no matter how much money you have you are not wanted here". When you are a person of color it doesn't matter where you live or how much money you have, racism can strike at any time.

The strategy of racism has always been aimed at destroying the family by cutting off the head then watch the body die. The strategy of cutting off the head is not new. However, what has changed is our lack of knowledge and understanding of the spirituality and culture that empowered us despite persistent attacks on our community. If spirituality and culture have been a protective force for thousands of years, can it still be effective in the twenty-first century? Other ethnic groups such as Latino Americans have been able to maintain and build their cultural institutions. These institutions reinforce their family bonds and cultural identity by using rituals, speaking their native language and maintaining a connection to their homeland. As a result, cultural identity is a factor for Latino families having a lower number of father-absent families. Studies have shown when ethnicity is considered, there is a significant difference between

African American and Latino families when it comes to father absence.

In the Latino community, 23% of the families are father-absent, compared to 57%, (and some reports has high as 72%) in the African American community. The statistics for father-absent homes in the Latino community are more in line with the statistics in the Caucasian community. Most Caucasian children live with two parents and almost two-thirds are currently being raised by both biological parents. Only one-quarter of African American children live with both biological parents, and the majority live in father-absent families. The above-stated statistics lead one to question, why do these differences exist? Also, what accounts for the similarity between Caucasian and Latino families, given that Latinos have a socioeconomic status like African Americans? One possible explanation may be the Latino community's ability to maintain its cultural identity.

This author asserts that cultural identity is a protective factor in the Latino Community. Cultural elements such as language, religion, and knowledge of ancestral homeland help protect the Latino family from factors that impact the African American family. If knowledge of one's culture is helpful for Latino families, then reconnecting the African American community to its cultural identity must be examined. Particularly, if it leads to a decrease in the number of father absent families.

Chapter Nine

What will it take to heal the family?

The African American community has reached a tipping point. We are at a point in time where 7 out of 10 children are growing up in a home without a father. For the first time in history, unconscious males are perpetuating father absence and threatening the survival of the black family as we know it. Without exposure to positive masculine energy, unconscious males who impregnate multiple women will continue to be a destructive force in the black community. If we do not address the impact of father absence, we risk another generation of boys growing up in poverty and entering the classroom to prison pipeline. Thousands of African American boys and men will be incarcerated during the most productive years of their lives. Their identity and way of thinking will be shaped by a system whose history of destroying black men dates back a thousand years. The system has studied the means of destroying lives with scientific precision and they continue to use research as a tool to incarcerate and mis-educate black people. Instead of our youngest minds being developed to maximize their potential they are shaped by an inhumane educational and prison system.

No species, human or animal can survive generations of males disappearing or acting as a destructive force in its society. Over time, a species or people can adapt but their social structure will be severely weakened and vulnerable without protective adults providing for their offspring. Father absence has reached the tipping point of being a crisis. African American men must take the lead in healing their sons and their families.

What will it take to heal black families? If we look at our culture, we will find the answers. There is an African proverb that says, "if you educate a man you educate an individual, but if you educate a woman you educate a nation". The wisdom of our ancestors is proven by research. Understanding, there are no differences in academic outcomes for father-absent children and children from two-parent homes when a single mother has the same level of education. We can conclude that educational opportunities empower single mothers and improve the lives of their children. If the desired outcome is to improve the standard of living for the poorest in our community, then men of color must take the lead in creating that reality. Our culture teaches us that we can educate a nation by uplifting African American women. If that is the case, then every black man must first look at himself to assess if he is part of the problem or part of the solution.

Self-awareness is the first step for African American men who choose to be part of the solution. Father-absent boys represent some of the most vulnerable children in our community. Men who are not conscious and self-aware will cause more damage. So, doing the work to raise your self-awareness is a prerequisite for working with father-absent children. Self-awareness fuels the desire to create positive change in your life and the children you encounter. It requires that you take an honest look at yourself and deal with the truth. An assessment of your strengths, weaknesses, and fears can facilitate growth if you take positive action. Your willingness to confront the truth so you can heal is exactly what you will ask father-absent boys to do. If you will not do it for yourself, then how can you ask anyone else to confront their truth.

The empirical wisdom of our ancestors also teaches us that work must be done by men with vision. It is written by our ancestors, "where there is no vision, the people will perish, but he that keeps the law is happy". Self-awareness, desire, commitment, and vision are required of men who educate the nation. The quote is not talking about man's law. Our ancestors are speaking about laws that govern all life and creation. These laws maintain a natural order throughout the universe. The laws are divine in their creation and the wisdom to use them has been passed on to us by our ancestors. They organize life on a cellular level to the most complex level. Because someone is ignorant of the law does not mean they can escape it. The law of reciprocity, vibration, and manifestation must be followed by all life to survive and thrive. If we are going to heal it must start with the "individual, and his awareness of how he is applying universal law to his life. The individual must choose if he will contribute to the wellbeing of others or think only of himself. Either way, he will live the reality he envisions. The vision starts with him; the individual, then extends to the woman, family, community, and nation.

What can you do as a conscious man to impact the lives of father-absent boys? First, is to have an awareness of self and the inner dialogue that creates your reality. It is the unconscious man who can inflict the most damage with his words and actions. Words have power! They can speak life or death into the world. As black men, we must examine what we are speaking into existence. We must be aware of the words we use to define ourselves and others in our community. Over years of practice as a psychologist, I have worked with hundreds of men and boys who were incarcerated. In my workshops, I asked the question, 'how many of you thought you would be in prison or dead before you were twenty-five'? Every time I ask the question almost all the men and boys raised their hands. They were unaware of how their inner conversation created the reality they were currently living. When they look back at their lives, they see the cause and effect of their thoughts and actions. As they awaken, the men understood their power to change their lives by being aware of the impact of their thoughts and actions.

The law of cause and effect is universal. It does not apply just to black men who are incarcerated. Its application is universal, no one is exempt. To facilitate healing, we all must examine the words we use to shape our reality, identity, and perception of others. If we agree that words have power, then we can learn to be more responsible when we use them. Ask the question, 'what language do I use internally and with other back men?' 'Do I limit or put myself down? Do I see myself or other men as niggers or dogs? Do I use words like, bitch or whore, to refer to black women or girls"? When you examine your way of speaking to yourself and others, it becomes clear how it affects your life. Do the words you use provoke anger or peace, do they lift you up or bring you down? When black men use words like "nigger," we are using words that were planted in our culture to destroy the collective consciousness of black people. But who planted these words in your consciousness? Are you conscious and free to remove words that were created to demean and destroy you? Some people would have you believe words like, "nigger, dog, bitch," can be redefined and take on a new meaning. To believe that a person would have to be unaware or misinformed about the traumatic effects of slavery and racism endured by people of African descent. Words have power beyond the physical world. They have energy and vibrations that take on a spiritual significance that can't be separated from its origin or creator. The origin of words like "nigger" carries a demonic spirit, as evidenced by the atrocities done by the people who created them. Where do the destructive words that we speak so freely come from and what is their intent? When you use words that have a demonic origin, they carry a mental and spiritual vibration that is part of the individual and the collective consciousness of a people.

Self-examination is an opportunity to pause to see how your internal and external conversation is impacting your life. I believe we are much greater than using the same language as the people who committed unthinkable crimes against humanity. The demonic language of racism was created to dehumanize people of color. It is through self-examination that you chose to exercise the power and freedom to remove those words from your consciousness. What is the cost of removing, "nigger, bitch, etc.", from the black man's vocabulary? Nothing! Something so simple, yet so powerful can't be stopped by government or racist institutions. It's up to the individual to decide he will no longer use words that destroy his mind, spirit and his family. Today, every man of color can declare his autonomy and create a new reality by simply changing his vocabulary.

The language of those who want to be mentally, physically and spiritually free must be different from the language of oppression. If change is going to happen, we must start with the head. That means that black men must look at themselves, start with cleaning up the language we use to identify ourselves and our people. We can transform our spiritual, physical and mental health by speaking a language of life and not destruction. When we do, the stress, anger, and fear will begin to heal us individually and collectively. The language we learned from those who did not know better or those who intended to harm us can be examined and improved. When we perceive ourselves, our women and children with respect and dignity, will words like "nigger and bitch", apply or have any meaning? How would removing dehumanizing words from our consciousness impact the lives of black people in America and the world? What message would it send if African American men took such bold action? It would start a cause and effect reaction that would change our lives, our families, the nation and the world. In time, the collective experience of black people around the world would be transformed.

Self-awareness is the first step in confronting the impact of father absence. It requires all black men to assess their behavior and be accountable for their actions. Through self-examination, you can assess if you are part of the solution or the problem. As part of the process of examination, I call on all men of color to delete the destructive words from their vocabulary and replace them with words that empower us to communicate, collaborate and heal our families.

When you talk to children who lived through verbal and physical abuse, they will tell you the words continue to cause pain long after the physical wounds have healed. Further evidence of the destructive force of words can be found when you examine public education and schools known as dropout factories. What language do policymakers and administrators use privately and publicly to describe the millions of black children in their system? Are they speaking words of life, hope, and optimism? Do their words create high expectations for our children that empowers them to achieve their dreams? Or do their words rob our children of their hopes and dreams? Research tells us millions of children throughout America are being robbed of their dreams before they finish elementary school. So, we must change the narrative starting with ourselves to make sure we are not unconsciously part of the problem. As we detox ourselves from dehumanizing words individually as men, we can start to do the work of lifting a nation.

In my personal and professional life, I have seen the change that happens when men elevate their internal dialogue. Several years ago, I had an experience with a group of young black males that reminded me of the power of inner dialogue. I was coming out of the Magic Johnson theatre in Harlem. When I turned the corner; I saw a young African American male standing on the hood of my new car laughing and joking with his friends. When I saw him, I stopped and said, "this kid is standing on my fucking car"!! I walked over to the group and told him to get down. I could see he was caught off guard. I looked at him and said, "there are people who will kill you for standing on their car. You need to be careful because for some people life is cheap!" We looked at each other in the eye. He could see I was sincere. I wanted him to be safe. The encounter ended with an apology and respect. But!! If I had turned the corner and said, "this nigger is standing on my fucking car", the outcome would have been very different. I would have been in attack mode and treated him differently. My demeanor and energy would have sent a different message. In my mind, the word, "nigger", would have dehumanized him. When the truth is, he was a young black male, someone's son who made a mistake. Because I didn't dehumanize him, he was open to learning from his mistakes. And I was reminded of the power of the internal dialogue. In my experience with black youth and men, when respect is given it is usually returned. It starts first with the individual being conscious of the inner dialogue he has with himself and expands out to the family, community, and nation.

The second thing we can do is connect with likeminded men to create a safe space for honest discussions about life, manhood, relationships, children and other important subjects. The goal is to form a network, a small group of friends where men can share information/resources, gain insight about themselves and benefit from the collective energy that only brotherhood can generate. As the saying goes "iron sharpens steel". As men of color, we often live in isolation. Living in isolation does not mean you have no social life. I'm talking about creating a space where you feel safe to speak about your inner world of emotions, dreams, and fears. It is the inner and most private areas of our lives that black men often feel isolated and unable to share. As boys, we are not socialized to master the world of emotions. We don't master the language that allows us to have meaningful conversations. Particularly, about our fears and most difficult times of our lives.

Creating a network and circle of men is an investment. It is an investment in your spiritual, emotional and mental growth. It is an investment that sharpens the mind and expands your knowledge. A group of strong men will also call you on your "bullshit". A man who is your brother will not allow you to live a façade and fake it through life. Every man should have men in their lives who are strong and care enough to tell them the truth. It is one of the greatest assets a man can have.

The group you are part of is a microcosm in preparation for the healing you can bring to the lives of people you encounter, particularly father-absent boys. How you choose to do that work is up to you. There are a million and one ways to be part of the solution. But, if you cannot commit the time and energy to take part in a group that facilitates healing, awareness, and power in your own life. Chances are you will not be able to commit to working with father-absent boys who are far more challenging.

Being part of a circle of men that genuinely care for each other's wellbeing is a powerful experience! I've been part of two of these groups in my lifetime. Both were extremely powerful and had a lasting effect on my life. The first was a group of ten men, all in our thirties. We started out talking about important issues, our lives, and relationships. Over time, we decided it was time to act in our community. We agreed to do a basketball tournament in a park that was taken over by drugs and full of thrash. Each of us contributed one hundred dollars and got a commitment from local businesses to provide matching funds, food, drinks, and T-shirts. With a budget of two thousand dollars and volunteered time, we conducted basketball clinics, hosted a tournament for kids and provided them with backpacks for school. None of which had been done in the community before. We started as a group of ten men, "iron sharpening steel," and ended up impacting the lives of children who felt forgotten in their community.

When likeminded men work together, they experience exponential growth. From an experience I had in my thirties, I gained lifelong friendships, self-awareness, knowledge, and experience. It was the springboard for working with men and father-absent boys for the rest of my life. From that experience, I moved on to organizing Rite of Passage Programs, helping to start an Afrocentric school for children, obtained a doctorate and worked with numerous organizations and agencies. It began, in part from the growth and support I gained from associating with men who were strong, supportive and positive.

The second time I experienced the power of brotherhood is when six lifelong friends and I committed to meeting at least once a month for a year. We met in each other's homes, prepared food, talked about life, marriage, divorce, fatherhood and being black in America. Even though we knew each other for years we never consciously created time and space to have powerful conversations as men. In those meetings, we experienced the full spectrum of emotions from laughter to pain. The whole time supporting each other's growth, strength, and power. I had no idea years later they would be one of the greatest sources of support at the lowest point of my life when I was going through my divorce. Again, the return on my investment was lifelong friendships, growth, knowledge, and healing.

If the group you create chooses not to do a community project like the one mentioned above, you still benefit from the exponential growth that comes from the experience. If it leads to strengthening your relationships, greater insight or help one person live a better life you have gotten a huge return on your investment. By growing in awareness, you become part of the solution. If your experience results in deleting the word "nigger, dog, bitch", from your vocabulary we all benefit from your awakening.

Third, sometimes a circle of men decides to expand their energy and influence out to the community. For this to happen there must be cooperation, collaboration, planning, implementation, and follow-up. These are all important skills and traits that are prerequisites for helping father-absent boys. It requires men to pool their resources, stop competing and put their egos in check. When egos are checked at the door anything is impossible! When the decision is made by the group to act, don't get weighed down by focusing on things you can't control. Choose to implement something that is doable, manageable and will make a meaningful contribution to the community. The goal is to make a contribution, not to change the world. All too often, we get bogged down by focusing on things we don't have, instead of the resources we do have. If your resources require you to scale back on the project, then do that. If the group needs more time, then push back the date. But do not get caught up in the planning phase hoping things will come together perfectly. When issues come up act quickly and address them before they become problems. That's the power of a small group of likeminded men. It is not part of the system that gets bogged down with politics and the slow process of making decisions. Your group is an independent part of the community that has decided to take action. Use the resources and contacts within the group and when you lack something, reach out to people to get the resources you need. Move forward with a sense of purpose and authority to improve your community. A unified group of black men with vision and purpose is a powerful force. Particularly, when they live in the community they are serving. It amplifies their creditability and power to bring about change in the community.

The experience I had with the first group placed me on the path of getting involved with the rite of passage programs for boys from father-absent homes. It is my strong belief that rite of passage programs can be a powerful intervention that can change the lives of young people. They draw on the history, culture, and spirituality of people of color. Historically, rite of passage was the indigenous system of education used by the people to prepare their children for adulthood. I believe that we must return to educating our children, either by creating independent schools or afterschool programs. The African American community must take ownership of developing the minds of their children. That means returning to the history, culture, and values that empowered our families and communities to thrive for thousands of years.

Developing rite of passage programs is a logical progression for a group of committed black men who want to have a long-term impact on father-absent boys. The focus of the program is to teach boys the skills and knowledge needed to transition into manhood. This is something that only black men can teach their children. It has been done for thousands of years. Taking ownership of educating our children is essential to protecting their minds and healing the family. Wherever you see people who have given up the right to educate their young, you will see people who are mis-educated to act against their own best interest. It is one of the first steps in colonizing a people. The Japanese people understood the importance of educating their children. After World War II, when Japan was negotiating the terms of surrender with the United States, one thing they refused to negotiate was the control of their educational system. The Japanese knew if they gave the enemy control of their children's education, they would be a conquered people. The Japanese surrendered their military. But they did not give up their greatest asset, the minds of future generations of children. The Japanese people rebuilt their country, maintained their culture, and became an economic power in the world.

If we are going to affect lasting change in the African American community, we must regain control of developing the minds of our children. We have seen generations of our children drop out of school into the prison system. African American men with vision have the power to change the future for generations of children. Rite of passage programs that develop a positive cultural identity and train boys to be men is a logical place to start. I will talk more about the power of rite of passage programs in the next chapter. But if you go through the three steps, (1) self-examination, (2) forming a group of likeminded men for growth and healing, (3) taking meaningful action in your community, then you have laid a foundation for changing lives. I encourage you to learn more about rite of passage as an effective way to improve the lives of father-absent boys in your community.

Chapter Ten

Cultural Rite of Passage as a Solution
to Save our Sons

Every culture has a definition of what it means to be a man, woman, and child in their society. The responsibility of adults is to teach the next generation their history, culture, knowledge, and skills needed to be a productive member of their society. Historically, every culture had some form of rite of passage that served as the educational system for transforming children into adults. It has been that way throughout human history, and it is no different today. What has changed is the creation of an institution that is expected to educate and serve fifty million children. A system that large will not and cannot be effective.

The size of public education in America guarantees there will be children who fall behind, fail and damaged by the system. The children that represent the upper and middle class in the system will receive the most funds and resources. They are the children who look like the powerbrokers and decision-makers. The children who fail and receive fewer resources will not look like the powerbrokers and decision-makers. According to research, those students will be poor children of color and most of them will come from father-absent homes. They are the students that have the greatest need for support and will benefit most from a culturally enriched curriculum such as a rite of passage programs.

If you and or your group decide to do a rite of passage program, there are things you should know and do before taking on the responsibility. You should avoid at all costs making a commitment that you cannot keep. You could cause more damage and distrust, particularly to children with a history of abandonment. So, part of the plan must account for time to train and educate the group. One of the mistakes adults often make is believing that coming from a similar background qualifies them to work with black children. That is a mistake! There is a set of skills and knowledge required to be effective when working with young people. Below, is an overview of the basic elements of a rite of passage experience and essential parts of planning a program for father-absent youth.

An Overview of Contemporary Rites of Passage Programs

African American rite of passage programs has been in existence in the United States for several decades. Over the past thirty years, there has been an increase in the number of programs implemented in the African American community. Broken down to its most basic elements, rite of passage involves four stages:

1); separation from the community,

2); preparation/instruction from elders,

3); demonstration of knowledge and self-discipline and

4); an induction ceremony celebrating the adolescent's transition to adulthood.

Grassroots organizations, churches, and community organizations such as Simba, 100 Black Men of America, Urban League, and other groups have implemented some form of rite of passage programs. The goal of the programs is two-fold. The primary goal is to provide the adolescent with the opportunity to be involved in structured activities that promote self-mastery, positive peer relations, ethnic pride, adult responsibility, and community involvement. The second focus of the program is designed to provide support to adolescents and their parents by increasing their awareness of resources and positive adults in the community. By increasing their awareness of resources, adolescents and their families can interact with responsible men and women in their community. The desired outcome is to protect youth from risk factors such as peer violence, substance abuse, academic underachievement, and teen pregnancy. These risk factors have been documented to be important issues in the lives of African American boys from father-absent homes.

Although there has been a steady increase in the number of rite of passage programs, there is a need for more research documenting the effectiveness of these programs. Grass root organizations, churches, and community organizations typically conduct their rite of passage programs independently and do not share information or data. Consequently, the diverse nature of the programs and their various curriculums make it difficult to replicate rite of passage programs on a national level.

Dr. Warfield-Coppock (1992) addressed the need for more research on rite of passage programs by conducting a study where she gathered data from existing programs. A comprehensive "rite of passage questionnaire" was developed and sent to 30 individuals across the country involved in the implementation of rite of passage programs. The questionnaire directed respondents to provide information about theoretical orientation, program standards, and future challenges their programs would face.

Out of thirty surveys mailed twenty were returned, which represented a response rate of sixty-six percent from a total of fifteen cities. Altogether, the respondents reported their organizations as having conducted 87 rite of passage programs and completing the initiation of 1,616 youth. The outcome data from the rite of passage questionnaires indicated that ninety percent of the respondents identified an Afrocentric or culturally specific theoretical approach. All the respondents felt that knowledge of self and culture was crucial to the future success of the youth in their programs. Other significant areas of focus were; (1); improved school achievement, (2); dissuading youth from early sexual activity, and (3); creating support networks for children from single-parent families.

The goals of these rites of passage programs appear to address many of the critical issues faced by father-absent children. However, there is a need to collect more information and outcome data to develop a best practice criterion that can be replicated by other community groups and organizations.

Considerations for Developing A Rite of Passage Program

Program Site: A neighborhood school, church or community center is an excellent site for a rite of passage program. These types of facilities tend to be centrally located, have a community identity, and usually already have programs for residents in the area. The classrooms or meeting rooms are convenient for workshops, conducting groups and classroom instruction. Neighborhood schools and community centers also have recreational facilities such as a gymnasium, game rooms, and swimming pools that can enrich the rite of passage experience.

Training the Trainers: Thorough and comprehensive training of the men is critical to a successful rite of passage experience. The social profile of the trainers should be that of an adult who is a person of integrity, responsible, culturally aware, respected by his family and community. Working with adolescents can be extremely challenging.

Therefore, trainers need to have the right temperament for working effectively with youth. The men should also be receptive to learning new skills and information to be effective trainers. Skills and knowledge in areas such as communication and group facilitation, child development, conflict resolution, and basic first aid are some of the essentials the group needs to learn.

It is recommended that an outside advisor with experience in rite of passage be consulted when a new program is designed and implemented. There are several advantages to using a consultant. First, the consultant can be objective in the selection and or screening of potential trainers. Second, the experienced advisor has completed his rite of passage and will be able to share his materials, knowledge, and experience with the group. Third, training of the trainers requires the men to complete a rite of passage experience as a group. This helps promote group cohesion and gives them experience in conducting cultural rites and rituals. The consultant is the person who guides the trainers through their rite of passage experience and identifies adults that might not be a good fit for working with youth. The consultant will also help the group overcome problems as they come up.

Program Development: The trainers should experience the same type of group process as the adolescents going through the rite of passage program. The consultant is the facilitator for the adult group. The group process is where the trainers begin to bond and assess the special skills, resources, and interests within the group. I recommend at least a 3-month training period. During this time the consultant assists the trainers in developing various parts of the curriculum based on the group's skills and special needs of the youth. If there is a need to focus on gang violence and activity the group must have knowledge of gang culture and the resources to address the problem. The same can be said if the emphasis is on teen fathers. The group must understand the concerns relevant to young fathers or any other area of focus. By participating in developing the curriculum, the trainers are more likely to take ownership of the program and see it through to its completion.

The foundation for a rite of passage program should be based on an African centered philosophy, rites, and rituals that have historical roots in our history and culture. I recommend the youth have two-hour sessions twice a week for at least six months to one year before completing the program. The first hour can be experiential (i.e. African rituals, team-building exercises, etc.) and the second hour used for classroom instruction. The youth should be assigned to age-appropriate groups (i.e. 13-15, 16-18 yrs.), group size should be 10-12 teens, and a good adult to youth ratio is 1 to 5.

<u>Parent Orientation:</u> The orientation provides an opportunity for parents and trainers to get to know one another. Parents play an important role in their youth's success by supporting and reinforcing the values and information taught in the program. The orientation also allows parents to get information about the experience of the trainers, ask questions regarding the Afrocentric philosophy, and voice any concerns about the program. The trainers should be prepared to give a presentation about their program and share their expectations with the parents.

<u>Community Service Project:</u> One of the assignments youth should be given is a community service project. The project helps to promote teamwork, personal pride and teaches the value of community activism. Projects such as neighborhood clean-ups, community gardens, and house repairs for the elderly are examples of some of the projects that can be considered.

<u>Induction Ceremony:</u> This ceremony is a community celebration that occurs after the youth have demonstrated an ability to master the skills, rituals, and information taught by the rite of passage trainers. The ceremony should include rituals and a community celebration with the youth who have demonstrated a commitment to the cultural values they've learned in the program.

Suggested Topics for Rite of Passage Program

African and African American History and Culture: There are many books, videos, movies and documentaries that have a wealth of information about Africa and African American history, culture and rituals. Each participant in the program should be given a book about a historical figure in African American history and be expected to do a presentation about the book. This will increase the youth's knowledge of African American history, as well as, teach him valuable communication and presentation skills.

Critical thinking skills: African American adolescents are bombarded with negative images portrayed in the media, history, and society in general. These images can negatively impact the youths' self-concept and desire to achieve. Learning critical thinking skills teaches young males how to look at unhealthy messages in the media and interpret them from a position of power. Discussing images that are portrayed in movies, the internet, magazines, video games, television, and music lyrics are some of the ways of sharpening the youth's critical thinking skills.

What to do when stopped by Police: Being stopped by the police can be a deadly encounter for African Americans. This is especially true for males who live in communities that are overpoliced and have fewer resources. Teaching our youth about their legal rights and how to effectively communicate and respond to police can save their lives. There are now community resources within law enforcement and non-profit organizations that can conduct a class on civil and legal rights and how to react when stopped by the police. This is vital information that all black youth should be taught.

Business & Entrepreneurship: A core principle of an African centered philosophy is creating and supporting an economic base in your community. Many young people today aspire to have their own business and be self-sufficient. This addresses a major problem in the black community as trillions of dollars continue to leave and enrich other communities. Helping students learn the basics of business and entrepreneurship empowers them to be self-sufficient. With technology, social media, and the internet, it is now possible for young people to have a business with very little start-up cost or investment. Entrepreneurship and business taught from an Afrocentric perspective should be part of every rite of passage program.

Nutritional health and wellness: African American men have higher rates of diabetes, high blood pressure, prostate cancer, and other diseases than White males in this country. Many of these diseases have been attributed to poor diets, high levels of stress and unhealthy lifestyles in general. The rite of passage experience provides an opportunity to teach youth about the importance of diet, nutrition, and exercise as a way of managing stress and preventing future health problems.

<u>Dealing with anger and the power of self-control:</u> Individuals who believe they can control their thoughts, emotions and actions feel empowered to direct the course of their lives. Poor anger management and impulse control is a major factor for young people dropping out of school and ending up in juvenile detention facilities. Participants in the program should discuss the consequences of anger and learn basic skills to express their feelings appropriately. The group can perform role plays to demonstrate effective anger management and communication skills.

The areas of focus mentioned above are suggestions for a rite of passage curriculum. Using an Afrocentric philosophy as the foundation allows you to focus on essential skills and information that will empower father-absent males. The goal is to introduce young boys to information that builds their self-confidence, self-discipline, self-knowledge, and competence in all areas of the curriculum. As important as the curriculum is, there's no substitute for building strong bonds with boys who need masculine attention. Remember, you are the most important part of the rite of passage experience. Your authenticity, sincerity, respect, and commitment are the greatest assets you can offer father-absent boys. Helping just one father-absent male lay the foundation for manhood has the potential to enhance the lives of generations of children. Father absence cannot be solved by politicians or any other institution. If we are going to heal the black family, it must start with African American men taking the lead.

Chapter Eleven

My Personal Experience
with rite of Passage Programs

Advocating for culturally specific interventions to address the impact of father absence on African American boys is based on years of personal experience with rite of passage programs. Before working on my doctorate in 1993, I studied African rites and rituals, as well as, designed, implemented, and consulted on many rite of passage programs. The programs were culturally specific, community-based, and served African American males 13 to 18 years of age. The adolescent males participating in the rites program typically lived in father-absent homes, were below average students, and were perceived by their parents to be a disciplinary problem in the home.

Young people living in large urban communities are likely to encounter rite of passage experiences throughout their adolescence and early adulthood. The issue is whether these experiences are structured or unstructured, prosocial or antisocial. For example, young people involved in street gangs undergo antisocial rites and rituals that value brotherhood, however; they also value violence, alcohol and drugs, and victimization of people in their community as well.

Involvement in antisocial rituals may include activities such as alcohol and drug use, fathering multiple children or engaging in violence to declare their manhood. The adoption of antisocial values can persist well into the youth's adult life, leading to incarceration, being a victim of violence or death. Gang affiliation is expected to be lifelong, which all too often is far too short. Consequently, the structured, prosocial rite of passage experience should not be viewed as a program for participants to complete and resume their individual lives without further guidance or support. It is an indoctrination into a community of conscious men. The goal is to further Afrocentric values (respect for self, women, children, elders, etc.), transform boys into men and minimize the negative effects of father absence. Done properly, a rite of passage program has the potential to be a transforming experience. You will have the opportunity to significantly influence the lives of African American males and lay the foundation for manhood and strong families.

As a rite of passage trainer, I have seen the transformation of father-absent youth who were incarcerated, failing in school and on a path of self-destruction. The adolescents who internalized Afrocentric values changed their negative thinking. They gave up the façade of being "hard" and adopted a different kind of toughness. The youth realized they could be mentally tough in the classroom. These hardcore teens learned to give up their fear of math and science and strive for academic success. They created a new vision of themselves. A vision that reflected Afrocentric values and a legacy of black excellence. With discipline and practice, they redefined what it meant to be "tough and hard." They realized black men can be tough in the classroom, corporate boardrooms and on the streets.

I have seen young African American males awaken to their untapped potential after completing a rite of passage program. The training caused a cognitive shift in young teens to see their fear of success as a weakness. As a result, the definition of being strong was redefined and applied to math, science and other subjects. Unfortunately, I have also seen some young people remain in a cycle of self-destruction. But changing the life of one boy can mean one less child growing up in a father-absent home.

Community rite of passage programs need more research that documents the effectiveness of their curriculum, training, and results. More research will allow trainers to identify best practices and standards that can be implemented nationally. This presents an opportunity for African American psychologists and sociologists to collaborate with community-based organizations in developing a rite of passage program based on empirical data and solid research.

Summary

According to Kids-Count.org data, in 2017, sixty-five percent of African American families with children under the age of eighteen are single-parent households. When you look at the research on father absence you see data reporting between 51% to 72% of African American children are living in father-absent homes. Boys from father-absent homes are at greater risk of living in poverty, developing a poor self-identity, dropping out of high school, and entering the classroom to prison pipeline. These studies suggest that millions of African American children will likely be affected by men who, for some reason, choose not to be a part of their child's life. Consequently, there is a critical need for effective interventions to address the specific needs of father-absent boys.

This book was written to inform the reader of the negative impact father absence has on African American boys. We have reached a tipping point that requires men to heal and work together to save a generation of black children. It is a call to action for men to do three things. First, to become more aware of the internal conversation that shapes their reality. Then decide to stop using words like "nigger and bitch," when referring to men, women, and children in our community. This simple action has the power to transform our families and communities. Second, to create a circle of men to communicate, collaborate, and have open/honest discussions that will heal the individual and empower the group. Third, use the power of the group to start a rite of passage program (or other positive action) to touch the lives of father-absent boys in their community. Impacting one father-absent boy can positively affect his life and generations of children.

This book draws on thirty years of experience working with African American men, children and families. African American men like all men want to protect and provide for their children. However, there are unconscious men in urban communities across America that perpetuate the cycle of father absence. The problem of father absence cannot and will not be solved by government or social agencies. It is within the power of the African American community to address the problem of father absence. Men must assume the lead role in saving our children. Only African American men can give father-absent boys the masculine energy and attention they need to complete the transformation to manhood.

References

Albrecht, S. L., Miller, M. K., & Clare, L. L. (1994). Assessing the importance of family structure in understanding birth outcomes. Journal of Marriage and the Family, 56, 987103.

Anderson, E. (1994). The code of the streets. Atlantic Monthly, 5, 80-94.

Astone, P. R., & McLanahan, S. S. (1991). Family structure, parental practices and high school completion. American Sociological Review, 56, 309-320.

Ballard, C. A. (1995). Prodigal Dad, how we bring our fathers home to their children. Policy Review, 71, 66-70.

Bandura, A. (1977). Social learning theory. In T. R. Murray, Comparing Theories of Child Development (pp. 231259). Wadsworth: Belmont California.

Bianchi, S. M. (1995). The changing demographic and socioeconomic characteristics of single-parent families. Marriage & Family Review, 20, 71-97.

Bianchi, S. M. (1990). America's children: mixed prospects. Population Bulletin, 45, 2-40.

Blumenkatz, D. G. & Gavazzi, S. M. (1993). Guiding transitional events for children and adolescents through a modem day rite of passage. The Journal of Primary Prevention, Ll..,.199-212

Courtney, M. L. & Cohen, R. (1996). Behavior segmentation by boys as a function of aggressiveness and prior information. Child Development, 67, 1034-1047.

Crooker, J. & Major, B. (1989). Social stigma and self-esteem. The self-protective properties of stigma. Psychological Review, 96, 608-630.

Delaney, C.H. (1995). Rites of passage in adolescence. Adolescence, 30, 891-897.

Fost, Dan. (1996). The lost art of fatherhood. AmericanDemographics,18, 16-19.

Hammond, R. W. & Yung, B. R. (1991). Preventing violence in at risk African-American youth. Journal of Health Care for the Poor and Underserved, 2,259-273.

Kids Count Data Center (2017). Single head of household, National data. Kidscount.org

Kunjufu, Jawanza (1984). Developing positive self-images and discipline in black children. Chicago: African-American Images.

McLanahan, S. & Booth, K. (1989). Mother-only families: problems, prospects, and politics. Journal of Marriage and the Family, 51, 557-580.

Manski, C. F., Sandefur, G.D., McLanahan, S. & Powers, D. (1992). Alternative estimates of the effect of family structure during adolescence on high school graduation.

Journal of the American Statistical Association, 87, 25-37.

McAdoo, H.P. & McAdoo, J.L. (Eds.) (1985). Black Children: social, educational, and parental environments. California: Sage Publications.

Mott, F. L. (1990). When is a father really gone? Paternal-child contact in father-absent homes. Demography, 27, 499517.

Mulkey, L. M., Crain, R. L., and Harrington, A. C. (1992). One parent households and achievement: economic and behavioral explanations of a small effect. Sociology of achievement: economic and behavioral explanations of a small effect. Sociology of Education, 65, 48-56.

Myers, H.F. & King, L. M. (1983). Mental health issues in the development of the Black American child. In G. J. Powell (Ed.), The psychosocial development of minority group children (pp. 275-306). New York: Brunner/Mazel.

Wade, J. C. (1994). African American fathers and sons: social, historical, and psychological considerations. The Journal of Contemporary Human Services, 54, 561- 569.

Warfield-Coppock, N. (1992). The rites of passage movement: a resurgence of African-Centered practices for socializing African American youth. Journal of Negro Education, fil., 471481.

Wilson, W. J. (1991). Another look at the truly disadvantaged.

Political Science Quarterly, 106, 639-656.

USA Today. (July 2017). Male teacher shortage affects boys who need male role models.

DR. GERALD C. HASSELL

CONTACT INFORMATION

Email: drgeraldhassell@gmail.com

Instagram: @drghassell